BUDDHIST PALI CHANTS

with

ENGLISH TRANSLATIONS

for use by students and in

MEDITATION RETREATS

Brian Taylor

道

UNIVERSAL OCTOPUS

Other Publications in the Same Series:

What is Buddhism?
Buddhism and Drugs
The Five Buddhist Precepts
Basic Buddhist Meditation
The Living Waters of Buddhism
Dependent Origination (Paticcasamuppada)
The Ten Fetters (Saŋyojana)
The Five Nivaranas (Buddha's Teaching of the Five Hindrances)
Basic Buddhism for a World in Trouble

Published by Universal Octopus 2016
www.universaloctopus.com

A catalogue record of this book is available from the British Library.

ISBN 978-0-9956346-2-6

CONTENTS

Pali is an Indo-Aryan language, current in Northern India at the time the Buddha was teaching and used by him.

It is the language in which his teaching is preserved in the Tipiṭaka, the sacred texts of Theravada Buddhism.

It was an oral language. It had no alphabet of its own.

The Buddha's teachings were not written down until the Fourth Buddhist Council in Sri Lanka in 29 BCE, in Sinhala script approximately four hundred and fifty-four years after the death of Gautama Buddha.

Pali was also written in Brahmi script as in the rock-cut edicts of Asoka in north-central India, dated to 250–232 B.C.

Pali has been transliterated into the alphabets of many languages.

I have used the Roman transliteration used by the compilers of the first Pali Dictionary for the Pali Text Society.

PRONUNCIATION

A is pronounced as "u" in English
"shut".
E is pronounced as "a" in "stake".
O is long as in "hope".
U is pronounced as "oo" in foot and "u"
in "put".
C as "ch" in "chair".
Double consonants. Both are pronounced: *dd* as in "good-dog" tt as in "cat-tail".

Some letters have diacritical marks to indicate variations in pronunciation:

Ṁ Ā Ñ Ī Ṭ Ṇ

Ṁ unvoiced nasal "ng" as in hang.
Ā long "a" as in father.
Ñ "ny" as in "canyon".
Ī long "i" as "ee" in sleep.
Ṭ lingual. With the tongue pressed against the palate.
ṬH as in "hot-house" never as in "thin".
Ṇ lingual with tongue rolled up.
Ū long "u" as "oo" in moon.

PRELIMINARY HOMAGE TO BUDDHA

NAMO TASSA BHAGAVATO ARAHATO SAMMĀSAMBUDDHASSA.

Honour to that Blessed One, the Worthy One, the perfectly Self-Enlightened One.

NAMO TASSA BHAGAVATO ARAHATO SAMMĀSAMBUDDHASSA.

Honour to that Blessed One, the Worthy One, the perfectly Self-Enlightened One.

NAMO TASSA BHAGAVATO ARAHATO SAMMĀSAMBUDDHASSA.

Honour to that Blessed One, the Worthy One, the perfectly Self-Enlightened One.

SALUTATION TO THE TRIPLE GEM

ARAHAṀ SAMMĀSAMBUDDHO BHAGAVĀ
The Worthy One, the perfectly Self-enlightened One, the Blessed One!

BUDDHAṀ BHAGAVANTAṀ ABHIVĀDEMI.
I salute the Buddha, the Blessed One.

SVĀKKHĀTO BHAGAVATĀ DHAMMO
The Dhamma, well-expounded by the Blessed One!

DHAMMAṀ NAMASSĀMI.
I pay homage to the Dhamma.

SUPAṬIPANNO BHAGAVATO SĀVAKASANGHO
Well practised are the Disciples of the Blessed One.

SANGHAṀ NAMĀMI.
I pay homage to the Sangha.

NAMO TASSA BHAGAVATO ARAHATO SAMMĀSAMBUDDHASSA
Honour to that Blessed One, the Worthy One, the perfectly Self-Enlightened One.

NAMO TASSA BHAGAVATO ARAHATO SAMMĀSAMBUDDHASSA.
Honour to that Blessed One, the Worthy One, the perfectly Self-Enlightened One.

NAMO TASSA BHAGAVATO ARAHATO SAMMĀSAMBUDDHASSA.
Honour to that Blessed One, the Worthy One, the perfectly Self-Enlightened One.

BUDDHĀNUSSATI
(RECOLLECTION OF THE BUDDHA)

ITIPI SO BHAGAVĀ ARAHAṀ SAMMĀSAMBUDDHO, VIJJĀCARAṆA SAMPANNO.

Just so. He is indeed the Blessed One, the Worthy One, perfectly Self-Enlightened, fully endowed with Vision and excellent conduct.

SUGATO LOKAVIDŪ, ANUTTARO PURISADAMASĀRATHI.

One who has gone well. Knower of Worlds. Unexcelled charioteer and trainer of men to be trained.

SATTHĀ DEVAMANUSSĀNAṀ BUDDHO BHAGAVĀTI.

Teacher of deities and men. The Awakened One. The Blessed One.

DHAMMĀNUSSATI
(RECOLLECTION OF THE DHAMMA)

SVĀKKHĀTO BHAGAVATĀ DHAMMO SANDIṬṬHIKO AKĀLIKO EHIPASSIKO.

Well expounded is the Blessed One's Dhamma. To be seen here and now. Timeless. Come and see!

OPANAYIKO PACCATTAṀ VEDITABBO VIÑÑUHITI.

Leading to (Nibbāna). To be known by the wise, each for himself.

SANGHĀNUSSATI (RECOLLECTION OF THE SANGHA, THE ORDER OF MONKS)

SUPAṬIPANNO BHAGAVATO SĀVAKASANGHO.
Well practised is the Sangha of the Blessed One's Disciples.

UJUPAṬIPANNO BHAGAVATO SĀVAKASANGHO.
Straightforward is the practice of the Sangha, the Blessed One's Disciples.

ÑĀYAPAṬIPANNO BHAGAVATO SĀVAKASANGHO.
The Sangha of the Blessed One's Disciples have practised properly.

SĀMĪCIPAṬIPANNO BHAGAVATO SĀVAKASANGHO.
The Sangha of the Blessed One's Disciples have practised correctly.

YADIDAṀ CATTĀRI PURISAYUGĀNI,
That is to say, the four pairs of men, (*Note 1*)

AṬṬHA PURISAPUGGALĀ.
the eight individuals. (*Note 2*)

ESA BHAGAVATO SĀVAKASANGHO.
This is the Sangha of the Blessed One's Disciples.

ĀHUNEYYO, PĀHUNEYYO, DAKKHINEYYO,
They are worthy of offerings, worthy of hospitality, worthy of gifts,

AÑJALIKARAṆĪYO.
worthy of respect.

ANUTTARAṀ PUÑÑAKKHETTAṀ LOKASSĀTI.
An incomparable field of merit for the world.

REQUESTING THE FIVE PRECEPTS

MAYAṀ BHANTE VISUṀ VISUṀ RAKKHANATTHĀYA TISARAṆENA SAHA PAÑCA SĪLĀNI YĀCĀMA.

May we, O Venerable One, ask to keep the five precepts, each individually and as a group, together with the three refuges.

DUTIYAMPI MAYAṀ BHANTE VISUṀ VISUṀ RAKKHANATTHĀYA TISARAṆENA SAHA PAÑCA SĪLĀNI YĀCĀMA.

For the second time, may we, O Venerable One, ask to keep the five precepts, each individually and as a group, together with the three refuges.

TATIYAMPI MAYAṀ BHANTE VISUṀ VISUṀ RAKKHANATTHĀYA TISARAṆENA SAHA PAÑCA SĪLĀNI YĀCĀMA.

For the third time, may we, O Venerable One, ask to keep the five precepts, each individually and as a group, together with the three refuges.

PAÑCA SĪLĀ THE FIVE PRECEPTS

1. **PĀṆĀTIPĀTĀ VERAMAṆĪ SIKKHĀPADAṀ SAMĀDIYĀMI.** (*Note 3*)
   I undertake to observe the precept to abstain from killing living beings.

2. **ADINNĀDĀNĀ VERAMAṆĪ SIKKHĀPADAṀ SAMĀDIYĀMI.**
   I undertake to observe the precept to abstain from taking what is not given.

3. **KĀMESU MICCHĀCĀRĀ VERAMAṆĪ SIKKHĀPADAṀ SAMĀDIYĀMI.** (*Note 4*)
   I undertake to observe the precept to abstain from misuse of the senses.

4. **MUSĀVĀDĀ VERAMAṆĪ SIKKHĀPADAṀ SAMĀDIYĀMI.**
   I undertake to observe the precept to abstain from false speech.

5. **SURĀMERAYA MAJJA PAMĀDAṬṬHĀNĀ VERAMAṆĪ SIKKHĀPADAṀ SAMĀDIYĀMI.**
   I undertake to observe the precept to abstain from intoxicating drinks and intoxicants which cause heedlessness.

BENEFITS OF THE FIVE PRECEPTS

IMĀNI PAÑCA SIKKHĀPADĀNI SĪLENA SUGGATIṀ YANTI.

These are the set of Five Moral Precepts. By means of Morality, beings go to the Celestial Worlds.

SĪLENA BHOGASAMPADĀ.

By means of Morality, beings achieve Wealth.

SĪLENA NIBBUTIṀ YANTI.

By means of Morality, beings go to Nibbāna.

TASAMĀ SĪLAṀ VISODHAYE.

For this reason, let them purify their Morality.

TRIPLE GEM THE THREE REFUGES

BUDDHAṀ SARAṆAṀ GACCHĀMI.
I go to the Buddha as a Refuge.

DHAMMAṀ SARAṆAṀ GACCHĀMI.
I go to the Dhamma as a Refuge.

SANGHAṀ SARAṆAṀ GACCHĀMI.
I go to the Sangha as a Refuge.

DUTI YAMPI BUDDHAṀ SARAṆAṀ GACCHĀMI.
For the second time, I go to the Buddha as a Refuge.

DUTI YAMPI DHAMMAṀ SARAṆAṀ GACCHĀMI.
For the second time, I go to the Dhamma as a Refuge.

DUTI YAMPI SANGHAṀ SARAṆAṀ GACCHĀMI.
For the second time, I go the Sangha as a Refuge.

TATI YAMPI BUDDHAṀ SARAṆAṀ GACCHĀMI.
For the third time, I go to the Buddha as a Refuge.

TATI YAMPI DHAMMAṀ SARAṆAṀ GACCHĀMI.
For the third time, I go to the Dhamma as a Refuge.

TATI YAMPI SANGHAṀ SARAṆAṀ GACCHĀMI.
For the third time, I go to the Sangha as a Refuge.

THE FOUR BRAHMA VIHĀRAS

Literally "the abiding places of Brahma" i.e. the most exalted states of mind. These are loving-kindness, compassion, sympathetic joy, and equanimity. They are not temporary emotions but sustained attitudes towards other beings which one has at all times. The following verses are chanted in temples and during meditation retreats.

LOVING KINDNESS (METTĀ)

LOVING KINDNESS TOWARDS YOURSELF

AHAṀ AVERO HOMI.

May I be free from enmity.

AHAṀ ABYĀPAJJO HOMI.

May I be free from ill-will.

AHAṀ ANĪGHO HOMI.

May I be free from suffering.

AHAṀ SUKHI ATTĀNAṀ.

May I myself be well and happy.

LOVING KINDNESS TOWARDS OTHER BEINGS

SABBE SATTĀ AVERĀ HONTU.

May all beings be free from enmity.

SABBE SATTĀ ABYĀPAJJĀ HONTU.

May all beings be free from ill-will.

SABBE SATTĀ ANĪGHĀ HONTU.

May all beings be free from suffering.

SABBE SATTĀ SUKHI ATTĀNAṀ PARIHARANTU.

May all beings preserve their own happiness.

COMPASSION (KARUṆĀ)

SABBE SATTĀ DUKKHĀ PAMUCCANTU.
May all beings be free from suffering.

SYMPATHETIC JOY (MUDITĀ)

SABBE SATTĀ MĀ LADDHASAMPATTITO VIGACCHANTU.
May all beings not be parted from prosperity or wealth obtained by them.

EQUANIMITY (UPEKKHĀ)

SABBE SATTĀ KAMMASSAKĀ.
All beings are the owners of kamma (action).

KAMMADĀYADĀ,
Heirs to kamma,

KAMMAYONI,
born of kamma,

KAMMABANDHU,
related to kamma,

KAMMAPAṬISARAṆĀ.
supported by kamma.

YAM KAMMAṀ KARISSANTI. KALYĀṆAṀ VĀ PĀPAKAṀ VĀ,
Whatever kamma they do, for good or for evil,

TASSA DĀYĀDĀ BHAVISSANTI.
of that they will be the heirs.

KARAṆĪYAMETTĀSUTTA
THE DISCOURSE ON LOVING KINDNESS

KARAṆĪYAMATTHAKUSALENA
He who is skilled in his own good
YAN TAṀ SANTAṀ PADAṀ ABHISMECCA:
and who wishes to attain that state of calm, Nibbāna, should act thus:

SAKKO UJŪ CA SUHUJŪ CA,
He should be able, upright, perfectly upright,
SUVACO CASSA MUDU ANATIMĀNĪ;
of pleasant speech, gentle and humble;

SANTUSSAKO CA SUBHARO CA;
Contented, easy to support;
APPAKICCO CA SALLAHUKAVUTTI;
having few or no duties, frugal;

SANTINDRIYO CA NIPAKO CA;
with senses pacified, prudent;
APPAGABBHO KULESU ANANUGIDDHO.
modest, not greedy or clinging to good families.

NA CA KHUDDAṀ SAMĀCARE KIÑCI
He should not do any slight wrong
YENA VIÑÑU PARE UPAVADEYYUṀ.
for which other wise men might later censure him.

SUKHINO VA KHEMINO HONTU.
May all beings be at ease and peaceful.

SABBE SATTĀ BHAVANTU SUKHITATTĀ.
May they be happy and secure.

YEKECI PĀṆABHUTATTHA,
Whatever living beings there are,

TASĀ VĀ THĀVARĀ VĀ ANAVASESĀ,
moving or not moving, without exception,

DIGHĀ VĀ YE MAHANTĀ VĀ,
whether long or great,

MAJJHIMĀ RASSAKĀ ANUKKATHŪLA,
or medium or short, small or big,

DIṬṬHĀ VĀ YE CA ADIṬṬHĀ,
seen as well as unseen,

YE CA DURE VASANTI AVIDURE,
those dwelling far or near,

BHUTĀ VĀ SAMBHAVESĪ VĀ,
those who are born and those waiting to be born,

SABBE SATTĀ BHAVANTU SUKHITATTĀ.
may all beings be made happy.

NA PARO PARAṀ NIKUBBETHA,
Let no-one deceive another,

NATIMAÑÑETHA KATTHACI NAṀ KIÑCI.
nor despise any person whatsoever, anywhere.

BYAROSANĀ PAṬIGHASAÑÑĀ,
In anger or ill-will,

NĀÑÑĀ MAÑÑASSA DUKKHAMICCHEYAṀ.
let him not wish any harm or wrong (to another).

MĀTĀ YATHĀ NIYAṀ PUTTAṀ,
Just as a mother, in the case of her own child,

AYUSĀ EKAPUTTAMANURAKKHE,
would protect her only child at the risk of her own life,

EVAMPI SABBABHUTESU,
even so, towards all beings,

MĀNASAMBHĀVAYE APARIMAṆAṀ.
Let him cultivate a boundless, infinite heart.

METTAÑCA SABBALOKASMIṀ.
Let his loving kindness pervade the whole world.

MĀNASAMBHĀVAYE APARIMAṆAṀ;
Let him cultivate a boundless, infinite heart;

UDDHAṀ ADHO CA TIRIYAÑCA,
above, below and across,

ASAMBĀDHAṀ AVERAṀ ASAPATTAṀ,
without any obstruction, without any hatred, without any hostility,

TIṬṬHAÑCARAṀ NISINNO VĀ
whether he stands, walks, sits

SAYANO VĀ YĀVATASSA VIGATAMIDDHO.
or lies down, as long as he is awake (without sloth).

ETAṀ SATIṀ ADHIṬṬHEYYA.
Thus, he should establish mindfulness.

BRAHMETAṀ VIHĀRAṀ IDHAMĀHU.
Here, they say, is the dwelling place of Brahma.

DIṬṬHIÑCA ANUPAGAMMA SĪLAVĀ
Not falling into wrong views, virtuous

DASSANENA SAMPANNO,
and endowed with insight,

KĀMESU VINEYYAGEDHAṀ.
he gives up attachment to sense-desires.

NA HI JĀTU GABBHASEYYAṀ PUNARETĪ TI.
Truly, he does not come again for repeated rebirth in the womb.

NOTES

Note 1 *The four pairs of men.*
The four stages of progress on the entry road to Nibbāna measured in terms of success in getting rid of the *Ten Fetters.*

1. Sotāpanna: 'stream-enterers'.
2. Sakadāgāmī: 'once-returners'.
3. Anāgāmī: 'non-returners'.
4. Arahant: 'worthy ones'.

Note 2 *The eight individuals.*
The same four as above, but further subdivided into pairs.

1. One practising to realise stream-entry.
2. *Stream-enterer* (one who has realised the fruit of stream-entry).
3. One practising to realise once-returning.
4. *Once-returner* (one who has realised the fruit of once-returning).
5. One practising to realise non-returning.
6. *Non-returner* (one who has realised the fruit of non-returning).
7. One practising to realise arahantship.
8. *Arahant* (one who has realised the fruit of arahantship).

Note 3 PĀṆĀTIPĀTĀ Literally: *make fall the breath.*
"Make fall" = kill.
"The breath" (of life) = those with breath.

Note 4 KĀMESU MICCHĀCĀRĀ Literally and originally: *misuse of the senses,* that is, any of the senses. Later, and especially recently, it has acquired the more limited meaning of *sexual misconduct,* which is variously interpreted.

Lightning Source UK Ltd.
Milton Keynes UK
UKHW012136031022
409859UK00003B/749

9 780995 634626